The Violinist

The Violinist

Translated from the Romanian by
Patrick Camiller

Calmo Rose

This book was printed in the United States of America.

Book editor for *The Violinist*: Denise Roman
Cover by: Vlad Cardei
All photographs are courtesy of Deniz Roman

The Violinist was originally published in Romanian under the title *Razboiul unui inocent* by Evenimentul Românesc. © Calmo Rose 2002.
Two previous English editions were published by Xlibris (2003) and World Drops Publications (2005).

DUENDE Books
Los Angeles, California, 2007
www.duendebooks.blogspot.com

To my daughter,
For encouraging me to go back in time
And bring forth, in written word,
These memories.

**Praise for the The Violinist,
originally published in Romanian under the title
Razboiul unui inocent [The Innocent's War]**

"*Razboiul unui inocent* is a book full of tenderness, lyricism, and humor; it has a remarkable power to evoke, with a different and refreshing tone, the emotional picture of the universal child caught up in the turbulent midst of dramatic times."

> Stefan Cazimir, Holder of the Chair of Romanian Literature, University of Bucharest, for *Adevarul literar*, 14 January 2003

"*Razboiul unui inocent* [is] a sensitive historical document with visible cinematographic virtues. The writing is permeated not only by life experiences, but also by the author's talent to find the best tone and word in order to complete a natural, apparently simple, narrative. The story intuitively inserts a tender nuance of irony, which accompanies the narrative discreetly, from the first page up to the surprising end. The product of a deep humanity and disquieting sadness, these recollections have marked not only the life of a child who is vacillating between an aggressed candor and a premature lucidity, but the life of an entire people."

> *Albina româneasca*, August 2002

"There are some books that oblige the reader to finish them in one breath. *Razboiul unui inocent* is one of them. . . . Calmo [Rose] reconstitutes with humor and gentle irony episodes from his childhood in Galati—[from] juvenile adventures, [to] the first feelings of love. . . . Recollecting an age of innocence profoundly marked by the burden of a tragic history, the author benefits from the adult's capacity of appreciating the past and from the writer's talent who, thus, transfigures a quotidian fact into a literary one. Razboiul unui inocent is not only a memoir, but also an opus of authentic literature."

> A. Oprea for *Diplomat Club*, December 2002

"[The author's] retrospective gaze is innocent and he has successfully managed to situate himself in the place of the child from his past. What is interesting in the book and pleases are not those scenes that reveal the horrors committed by the Romanian authorities against the Jews, but the simplicity and naturalness of the remembrances, which are replete with humor. . . thus proving the author's qualities as a story teller."

România libera, 13 September 2002

"Situated in a present time of recollection, the author lends the narrator something from the adult's self-irony. As a result, the child sees himself and the others with a pronounced distinctiveness. Overall, the book suggests a smart and amusing perspective on some dramatic realities, succeeding, in a paradoxical way, to convince us of the nightmare lived by the Jewish community in times of madness. The story-teller, thus, gives a helping hand to the memoirist as they achieve together a book of great intellectual satisfaction."

Ion Cristoiu, from "Foreword" to *Razboiul unui inocent*

**Praise for the English version of
The Violinist**

"With sadness and humor, Calmo Rose describes the life of a family of Jewish refugees who leave Bucharest after the January 1941 pogrom to escape to the Soviet Union. Interned in Galati (on the Danube) for the entire duration of the war, the Rose family endure the humiliations that were commonly applied to the Jews from the Regat [the Old Kingdom of Romania], including forced labor, beatings and threats. The father will survive while laboring in almost impossible working conditions, producing de-luxe shoes for his guardians, while his son will use his passion for the violin and his optimistic nature to transcend this terrible ordeal . . . . Unlike many other Jews from the Regat, Calmo Rose and his family were lucky. They survived the war without being massacred or deported."

Radu Ioanid, Director, International Archival Programs Division, Center for Advanced Holocaust Studies, United States Holocaust Memorial Museum, Washington D. C.

"I read Calmo Rose's [*The Violinist*] with great personal and professional interest. It is a moving and well written account of a child prodigy, reflecting the emotional turmoil of a pre-adolescent's unfulfilled love amidst the suffering of his family in the wake of Marshal Ion Antonescu's anti-Semitic policies in wartime Romania."

Randolph L. Braham, Distinguished Professor, Emeritus, Director of the Rosenthal Institute for Holocaust Studies, City University of New York

"Like Aharon Appelfeld, [Calmo] approaches the Holocaust indirectly, through the remembered voice of a child, the better to understand that terrible time. The story is terrifying, touching, and in places also very funny. I especially appreciated young Calmo's passion for Luta who came to represent all that was unattainable, beautiful, secure, and serene during that monstrous and murderous time."

Robert Melson, Professor of Political Science, Purdue University, author of *False Papers: Deception and Survival in the Holocaust*, and child Holocaust survivor from Poland

Chapter One

Sometimes I feel as if I am sleepwalking through past events of my life, and now and then I can even believe I have lived them. It is not the I of today, though. It seems like someone else, a kind of double upon whom I gaze with reverence, sometimes with tears in my eyes.

I turn my head toward distant horizons and climb the steps of a never-ending staircase. I really do see my one sovereign world, the world in which I believe; it is real, even though it no longer exists.

At other times it is as if I am leafing through a large, thick book, a kind of bible, whose every word evokes different happenings and feelings buried deep inside me and now brought to the surface by I know not whom. Actually I cannot tell what the book is; it might suddenly seem more like a volume of stirring tales, either sad or cheerful, or else an album of sepia-tinted photographs taken by the dim light of a gas lamp or a smoking candle.

Certain sounds and smells arouse me and call to mind various flowers, making me curious to wander among my memories. A snatch of a tune or a pleasant sound, a sudden peal of laughter, the flapping of a sparrow's wings, a shouting child, the angry bang of a car's exhaust. . . . And yet, I feel just like a stranger searching for his birthplace who, having discovered it again or found it changed from how he knew it, tries to recreate it from his imagination.

It is night, and soon we shall be leaving the ship of the millennium. I am listening to the lament of a violin, whose trembling voice rises somewhere in a nearby apartment. Ancient images flood into my head and bring back that moment long ago . . .

But look how my thoughts are rambling, and even in these recollections I would not like to upset Luta. Ah, how many years have gone by! The face of that little girl appears before my eyes, eight or nine years old as I myself roughly was at the time, with soft fawn-like eyes that fascinated me and looked from behind long lashes at the wonders of the world. And I liked to think that I was one of those wonders! How did I look? A midget, snub-nosed and slightly freckled, mightily ambitious, bored with the violin lessons of my Bessarabian teacher Katevman or his successor from Galati, the good-natured Mr. Leibovici.

I remember that I first came across her on my way to school and was completely bowled over. Scarcely had I distinguished her features when my prankish yet innocent heart began to leap in my breast, painfully shaking me to the core. Instead of finding my way to school, I kept following her until she eventually disappeared into a Galati courtyard. A while later, I glimpsed her in a little draper's shop on Strada Tecuci, together with a smart good-looking woman who was evidently her mother. Again I trembled at the sight of her. She was beautiful, magnificent—a true goddess. The world around me began to take on new shapes and colors, more lively, more enticing, more ardent. Once more I followed her home, somewhere on Strada Brâila.

I began to dream of her at night, to look for her on imaginary streets so that she would smile at me or at least favor me with a glance.

I no longer ate a thing and became as thin as a rake, driving Mother to despair. Obsessed with her face—I never imagined she had a body as well—I went to school in a trance, as if pulled along by a thread. In class it was hard to return from afar when the teacher suddenly turned and addressed me. I was dreaming with my eyes wide open.

My school friends—Dulce, Ciuraru, Spielman—were terribly sharp and soon found me out. They knew everything, understood everything, in a way that I still find amazing. Dulce would sit beside me on the corner of Strada Brăila, eager to allay my suffering. He took on an air of gravity and compassion, although that was not his real nature—for he was a kind of classroom jester who loved nothing so much as fooling around. We used to wait hours on end, beneath rain, wind or snow, for Luta to appear at the fern-covered balcony on the first floor of her house. I longed only to see her. Sometimes the fairy queen would appear, sometimes not.

Our class swot, an evil red-haired boy called Spielman who seemed to draw out the words in his mouth and who was spurred on by his mother to fight me for top place, used to drive me crazy with his talk:

"I saw her on the arm of a German in the public gardens, along the shore of Lake Brates."

I calmed down only when I found out that she had been to school, closely guarded by a maid.

Even today, after a whole lifetime of shocks and hardships, a candle still burns for her in the chaster part of my soul. I still see her smiling face just as I knew it in Galati, in the dramatic circumstances of the forties.

They were hard times. By no means did they augur well for the troubled love of a kid who had just finished first grade at Bucharest and was trying to come to terms with the new life that his family desired yet was unable to achieve. The frontier with the Soviet Union had been abruptly closed, and anyone caught secretly crossing the Danube on a moonless night, in a fishing boat or makeshift vessel, was arrested, soundly beaten, and "sent on their way"—that is, back to where they had come from.

I see myself again on the slow train from Bucharest to Galati in that winter of 1941—a winter of heavy snowfalls followed by terrible frosts. I am sitting among dirty suitcases that my father, a luxury cobbler (sorry, I mean "shoemaker," as he pedantically liked to be called—but more of him later), has carefully tied up with strips of flax. My mother Ana, a skilled dressmaker who has worked for years in a sweatshop on Calea Vãcãresti, looks fearfully around the compartment to make sure that we have not been followed by a Hungarian called Karol, a monster of a man to whom Father, just the evening before, has sold the shoemaker's shop with all its tools, lasts and other contents, probably "forgetting" to tell him that he has not paid any of the last quarter's taxes. It is this man who has been angrily scouring the railway station in the hope of laying hands on us.

When the train starts to puff lazily forward, Karol's head appears in the corridor right in front of our compartment; his eyes skim over us without realizing who we are, until finally he takes a running jump off the train and stands on the platform cursing to high heaven in Hungarian.

Only then did we breathe a little more easily. Father's ghostly-pale face brightened, and he told us that from now on, with God's help, it would all be plain sailing as we headed for a new life, better for the poor, juster and without persecution for the Jews.

I had not often seen Father with such a fearful expression. He was a courageous, straightforward sort of person, who had been through many trials in his life. He, trooper Moshe, had been called up into the Romanian army for months at a time, in 1938, 1939 and 1940, at Sighetul Marmatiei, Apahida and Oradea, in the 2nd "Mountain Corps" Battalion, from which he would return once a month or so with a load of army bread and a chunk of bacon that we made last until his next appearance. The shoemaker's shop was closed: it no longer produced anything, and the only worker loyal to the family, Gică—a country lad with a heart of gold who had learned the trade from Father and, I am sure, was very fond of us—had been conscripted and sent to the frontier with Hungary. The Transylvanian question was stirring people up a great deal at the time.

Even so we managed to get by from day to day, until a new law "discharged" the Jews as unworthy to defend the ancient Romanian lands on which they too had lived for hundreds of years and always done their duty to King and Country. This, I repeat, was in the years 1939-1940.

I was just seven years old and the time had come for me to be sent to school. Not far from our home on Strada Alexandru Moruzi Voievod, nearly opposite the Stone Cross area that was a kind of squalid Bucharest version of Montparnasse, I had started enrolling at a primary school on Strada Lucaci about which Father had heard all kinds of wonderful things from a customer of his.

"It's a really nice school that gets good results," he was told. "Study there and you come out a man."

So off I went hand in hand with Father, in clean clothes, shiny shoes and a starched white shirt, while Mother watched us with tears in her eyes, hopeful but also—for reasons I did not understand—deeply worried. We presented ourselves at the school administration and quietly waited with other parents for our turn to be called.

Father, in his talkative, jokey style reminiscent of a character from Sholom Aleichem, addressed the school secretary, a small and seemingly honest man.

"I've brought our offspring along for you to give him a proper education. He's my boy. He even plays the violin."

"And what might your offspring's name be?"

"Calmo Rose."

"Rose—what kind of name is that? Is it Jewish, perhaps?"

"Yes." Father tried to put a better gloss on things. "I've just come back from many months in the army, on the Hungarian frontier."

"Okay, okay, but I can't do anything for you. We haven't any room for Jews in our school. We're not allowed . . . "

"And might I ask why you aren't allowed? Have we got the plague or something? I am a Romanian citizen, after all. My father-in-law Avram is a maimed war veteran, decorated by the king with the Order of Military Valor. He lost his legs at the battle of Mārāsesti fighting for our country's independence."

"Orders from above, from the ministry. I've got nothing against you. It's the instructions we've been told to follow."

"But why won't they let me go to school with my best friends, Vali and Dodu? What have they got against us?" The question slipped into my head, seeming to vindicate Mother's anxiety about my first trip to school. In any event, they did not admit me.

This was one of the many serious anti-Semitic measures introduced by the successive regimes of Goga-Cuza, the Iron Guard, Horia Sima, and Marshal Antonescu.

It was the first time I saw Father looking white as a sheet. Since newspapers never entered our home and our relationship with society was largely mediated through shoes, my parents were not exactly au fait with what was happening in the world. Nor did they feel in their own existence other crimes of that period such as the expulsion of Jews from the legal profession and the Association of Romanian Writers, or the official sponsorship of racism in the form of a *numerus clausus*.

The second occasion on which I saw the paleness of anxiety on Father's face was just before the Iron Guard revolt in January 1941. One evening Mr. Bercovici, a schoolteacher who was always wearing down his heels and had therefore become a frequent visitor to our house, rushed in to tell us of some suspicious activity at the Iron Guard center at "Làzàrescu," a little metal factory at the top of Strada Tepes. "They'll come out at night and kill us all. There'll be a bloodbath, a pogrom." Father frowned and did not give much credence to what our well-wishing neighbor had reported. To Mother he remarked: "What would they do to us—after all, I'm a soldier just back from frontier duty. The way our people exaggerate!"

Yet barely half an hour had passed when another neighbor, Vasile Pârgu, crossed the threshold of our house; he was a carter at the local timber yard, a poor fellow like ourselves, who ran around all day long to earn his morsel of bread, and with whose children I used to play "cops and robbers" every afternoon. He knew that Father had done months of military service in Oradea, but he did not know that Father was Jewish. And so this Uncle Vasile asked Father to go with a nest of Iron Guardists the next day to smash up some Jewish stores. That was what Horia Sima had asked them to do.

"Let's go along too, Misule," he said to Father. "Maybe we'll come away with something for ourselves."

"How could I do something like that, Vasile old man? Don't you know I'm a Jew?"

"God strike me down if I knew! Why, you've just been on frontier duty for months on end." After thinking it over for a few moments, he continued:

7

"Well, you'd better come to my place tonight. Those people at 'Lăzărescu' have got lists of everyone"—he was embarrassed to utter the word "Jews" again. "It'll be safer for you and the boy."

Uncle Vasile the carter had been as fond of me as of his own children since he had made my "acquaintance" a good few years before, when I had been four or five years old. I liked to strut about in the street, clutching a willow twig in my hand and amusing the whole neighborhood with loud snatches of verse that I had picked up from somewhere or other.

> When I see you red of hair
> I puff up like a rooster.
> I giddy you up
> You giddy me up
> We both of us . . .
> Giddy each other up.

The general amusement at these lines was all the greater in that it was an innocent child delivering them in a street near the Stone Cross district, the district of "monkeys," as Mother called the half-naked girls who hung around there.

There was another family event, of which only Uncle Vasile had any knowledge.

One evening he witnessed an incredible scene in our workshop: I, wearing a pair of women's knickers up to my neck, was marching up and down as Father wildly sang the March of the Mountain Corps. In his hand was a leather belt, and he lashed out with it whenever I failed to keep time.

"What on earth is going on?"

"I'm teaching the little one to stop doing it in his pants. I'll make him parade in women's knickers, so that he feels ashamed and remembers me for the rest of his life."

Uncle Vasile saved me from Father's military instruction, at least on that occasion when he was on leave and evidently marked by the army spirit, as well as by the fact that I was still doing it in my pants. Mother stood in the doorway and cried, unable to tolerate the punishment that was being meted out to me. Father had directly identified the "crime" one evening when, after my return from play, he had taken me in his arms to kiss me and noticed that I had a horrible smell. After touching my bottom and realizing what had happened, he immediately let fly at me:

"You little shitbag! Are you still tormenting your mother at your age?"

But to return to the story: on those terrible nights of 21, 22 and 23 January 1941, when the Iron Guard's criminal revolt left a number of Jews hanging from meat hooks and wrecked dozens of Jewish stores, our family found shelter with that decent neighbor, Vasile Pârgu, who loved other people and who was determined to save from destruction a Romanian soldier's family of Jewish origin.

We were lucky. All that happened to us was that some Iron Guard symbols and a six-pointed Star of David were scratched onto our shop's only street window. They were stamped in my mind forever, those prison-like bars of the Iron Guard symbol.

Fear and anxiety became a daily presence. News came thick and fast about the pogrom in Iasi, the "death trains," and all the other terrifying things that began when General Ion Antonescu came to power and took the Iron Guard under his wing, those "dear children" of his who used to wear pistols at the waist for obvious purposes. That winter, Father would come and go stealthily through the back door into the yard. By tacit agreement our customers too used that entrance when they came for their shoes to be soled or heeled: Mr. Ionescu from the bank, Mr. Angelescu from the grocery store, who sometimes abused our delicate situation and forgot to pay; Mr. Vută from the soda-bottling shop, who was now addressing us with a changed, harsher tone; and Mr. Aronovici the lawyer banned from the Bar—each and every one. They protected us from any calamity. Such people!

Chapter Two

"Ana," Father said to Mother on one of the very difficult days that followed, "get everything together for a journey, because tomorrow evening we're leaving for Russia. I've heard that no one there is looked on as a Jew, that everyone is equal. Our boy will be able to learn and to end up with a degree"—which I think, for Father, was the equivalent of being an English lord. "As for me, I can even become a city councilor." That, in his view, was the highest anyone could rise with just two classes at primary school; it was his dream of maximum advancement, may God forgive him!

There is no point in my saying any more about the hopes of other passengers on that slow train for Galati, most of whom were dejected artisans or small traders. Among them was Simcas, a doctor from Timisoara, and Gloter, a student who in later years became the well-known Preda on Romanian

Radio, and who, having to choose between a fascist regime and the Soviet Union, preferred the Red neighbor for the sake of survival.

"Even in Palestine the British and the Germans are killing us; the Arabs in Palestine hunt us down—that's more or less what is rumored." (Unfortunately the rumors proved true exactly a year later, in February 1942, when a convoy of 700 people left on another train, this time from East Station to Constanta, and eventually embarked on a British ship, the Struma, that was sunk by Germans in the Bosphorus.) "Russia is the land of freedom for everyone. There is even a region governed by Jews, in Birobidzhan."

What did we know in those days?!

A sweet euphoria rose from among the tired-looking trunks, suitcases and tightly bound packages, in which lifetimes of toil were now condensed.

I slept a good few hours with my head on Mother's lap. "Sleep, little one, who knows what lies ahead."

Suddenly the train stopped with a lengthy screeching of brakes. The harsh voice of a gendarme woke me up.

"People from Galati should move towards the locomotive; Jews, go to the storage sheds behind the station."

It was hard to make out the platform, as it was covered with shiny snow. Bitter cold lashed our faces as soon as we stepped off the train and began dragging ourselves and all our pauper's belongings to the place indicated by the gendarme; he had meanwhile sprung to life and kept pushing us with his rifle butt. Our whole wagonload of men, women, children and old people tumbled into a large shed made of wooden planks, and each moved as quickly as possible to find a little corner for himself. Within a few minutes the floor was a human space, an area set aside for poor wretches. Fear of death had burrowed deep inside us all. "What if they come and shoot us?" The collective memory still harbored images of the innocent victims of the Iron Guard pogrom, as well as of other injustices and humiliations of recent years.

A few minutes were all it took for the shawls, rugs and blankets firmly marking each family's "living space" to be whisked out of the various suitcases. Everyone was striking out on all sides, with shouts and tears, pushes and shoves, children's whimpering and old people's groaning, but also with stern appeals for reasonable behavior from male heads of families. How could there have been any question of reasonable behavior in such conditions?

Worst off were those beside the shed's large wooden doors, whose cracks allowed the blizzard outside to roar pitilessly over them.

Yet, as if by a miracle, we did see the calm, reasonable behavior that had been requested just as the hubbub was starting. Single people or young couples without children had to move closer to the "Gate of Hell" at the entrance, while the weakest or those closest in age to life's end occupied the places left vacant on the "lawn."

We eventually found ourselves amid the bustle on one of the plank walls, which Father quickly muffled with a small blanket as some protection against the blasts.

After an hour in the darkness, now and then pierced by someone striking a match to find a child's pot or to check whether a loved one was feeling ill, a sudden stillness descended that was broken only by variously pitched snores, muttering sounds, and an occasional whimpering or shrieking from the depths of slumber. Towards morning, the shed was shaken by the bellowing of a gendarme.

"All males must show their travel documents and identity papers to the sergeant—at the other end of the station."

The order was carried out, and that is how we discovered shortly afterwards that we were to be kept in the station shed at Galati until further instructions came "from above."

For ten days, in that pathetic station outhouse which had once held stores of cement sacks, we endured nothingness and icy cold, the groans and shouts of the old and sick, the pains of rheumatism sufferers and children ill with untreated pneumonia.

In accordance with ancient custom, "negotiators" were found to bargain with the police sergeant, who, for a price, would release groups of two or three men at nightfall, keeping their families behind as a guarantee of their return. These men then desperately scoured the town to buy something to put in people's mouths, trading various objects because there was less and less money available.

Father, too, handed over a few dozen lei for the right to purchase something to eat. Moreover, in return for a pair of newly made shoes of which he had liked to boast, he received a primus stove whose flame warmed many a frozen hand—and, more important, many a poor soul.

Together with that glow appeared a ray of hope, a belief that some things were still possible.

In those days of fear and confinement, it was given to me to begin unraveling some of the world's great mysteries, with the heart and mind of a nine-year-old child.

Next to us on the area of the carpet, a swarthy man with wavy hair "lived" on an open suitcase extending onto a piece of rug. And by a miracle, without uttering a word between his closed lips, he managed to "foul-mouth" the world around him.

"Death to the Germans! Hitler is a swine! Let him feel what we feel now!"

It took my breath away. Yet the ventriloquist—which is what I was told he was—suddenly found himself called upon from all sides to put a stop to it. "What will you do if there's a squealer among us?" "Cut it out, you idiot! Do you want us to end up on a hook in the slaughterhouse?" Such were the voices of fear and experience that came from the crowd.

Pummeled by local "public opinion," our neighbor continued to present his repertoire—but more softly, for my ears alone, since I was the only one who sat gaping with admiration. One jolly dialogue that he had composed himself gave me new heart.

"How are you feeling?"

"Fine, thanks. I hope Antonescu is, too, with God's help."

"Who's he—Antonescu?"

"A kind of benefactor of the Jews, as you can see."

Father put an end to the other questions that were forming in my mind and calmed me down.

"That's not for your ears; it means big trouble. Don't get mixed up in any more of that! You never know who you're dealing with."

And he added, for the benefit of the ventriloquist:

"That goes for you too, if you don't mind me saying so."

On another part of the new "territory" defined by the family carpet, an older man with black turtle-shell glasses was nearing the end of his days, for some reason addressed with respect by his neighbor on the other side. He looked at me with gentle eyes that inspired confidence and gave me courage.

During those days a question kept going around my head. What have the Germans got against the Jews that makes them want to kill us all? I asked him that in a low tone, so that Father would not hear.

"Listen, my pet, the Jews are good: they're even better than many Germans, and the Germans can't stand that. I'm telling you, their great poets and musicians are Jews: Heine, Schiller, Mendelssohn-Bartholdy, Fritz Kreisler. .

. . Germans who want 'living space' for themselves, for their 'pure,' 'superior'

race, also say that there are too many Russians or Slavs—which is why they

want to pillage and occupy their land and to spread Greater Germany far and

wide. It's called the Drang nach Osten. Right now we're trying to cross over to

the Russians, and since the Russians are Communists people are calling us

Communists too. But we are running away to Russia to save our lives."

That was when the word "Communist" first entered my consciousness.

Roughly three carpets from ours, towards the corner of the shed, was

the territory of a blanket maker from Oradea, a tall and handsome man with

thick dark hair falling over his face, who had come to these parts together with

his wife, Eva. I am not sure why, but I felt drawn to look at her face for a long

time, without any particular emotional charge. It quite simply made me feel

rested to gaze at her with admiration—as I might at a rose or a book with nice

pictures.

But, heavens, what I glimpsed one day made such an impression on

me! In the semi-darkness of that room, the woman proceeded to undo her

blouse revealing two pear-like breasts upon which her red hair flowed down in

streams.

I instinctively fixed my eyes on her to see what she would do next.

Having checked that no one was watching, she nimbly eased down her skirt and

then her panties. For a few seconds she stood there stark naked.

I was thrown into turmoil by the beauty of the image that I was

beholding for the first time. I do not know what troubled me so profoundly,

but I could perhaps sense—also for the first time—that I belonged to the male

sex.

Beautiful Eva hurriedly dressed with the same stealth, apparently

satisfied that she had finally been able to change her clothes after so many days and nights of confinement. Then she glanced at me for a moment, focusing her deep green eyes and seeming to ask for my discretion. I lowered my eyes in shame.

But there were two other witnesses to the scene—Mother and Father—who were whispering between themselves. Mother, looking intrigued, eventually broke the silence:

"Why do you gawp at women like that? Aren't you ashamed of yourself?"

I was the target of her words—but also Father. He found a way out easily enough:

"Leave the kid alone. Do you want him to grow up a dunce, like Farfolah, the tailor's son? At thirty he's still a 'spinster' because of his mother, and his face is covered with spots and pimples. What do you know about these things?"

I "lived" in that wretched shed for ten days. I was no longer interested in any of the human fretting and flailing that I saw there, although the privations affected me as well. My mind and my eyes kept seeking out Eva, who—to cap it all—seemed to be magically aware of my attention and offered me two more evening "shows." This especially satisfied my watchful father; he was in a good mood and had some cash in his pocket, as he had sold the last pair of shoes from his collection during one of his excursions for food.

One evening, when a thick carpet of large powdery snowflakes covered the landscape, the sergeant came rushing in and released us. His words were brief and to the point:

"Clear out of here, any way you can, round the back of the station. I want this shed empty five minutes from now. Cement is arriving for the garrison. It's an order!"

The spotless white of the snow submerged every habitation and seemed to have banished all human life from the streets that lay before us. In front of the station, we threw ourselves into a sledge with wide runners drawn by a couple of sturdy horses that never stopped snorting, their driver wrapped from head to foot in a gray fur coat that let us see no more than his red face lashed by the blizzard. We told him we were in a great hurry.

"Where to? What's the address?"

Address? What address could we have had, lost as we were in an unfamiliar snowed-up town that was alive for us only through the strands of chimney smoke slowly scattering at the pace of the wind?

We spent three hours of that giddy night under the whip of the icy north wind, trying to find accommodation at the various addresses suggested by a driver who more or less understood the situation we were in. Everywhere we knocked, however, at street gates or front doors, no one deigned to come out and ask us what we wanted. No one so much as opened for us.

At last fortune did smile on us. On Strada Lapusneanu in the center of town, at a spot where a solitary lamp hanging near the statue of Costache Negri gave out a little more light, someone was struggling alone through the drifting snow. As if aware of who we were and what we wanted, he climbed onto the sledge beside the driver and whispered something in his ear. After a while longer in the darkness of night—I could no longer feel my fingers and toes—we drew up in front of Strada Columb, No. 72. A hand-to-hand tussle eventually got the better of the tall wooden gate rendered stiff with cold, and we passed a series of little huts each the height of a man arranged on either side of a rectangular courtyard.

Still feeling harassed by cold and fear, we stepped into a room slightly larger than a dovecot that held no more than one covered wooden bench and a gas lamp with a box of matches beside it. The terrible cold had already clouded our vision. And now our breath gushed out as hot steam in the icy cave-like room.

We put on the whole suitcase of clothes and lay on the bench huddled against each other beneath a rough goatskin blanket, while the dim lamp mocked our fate with its good-for-nothing wick.

A choking smell of unburned gas forced us to open the door by a hand's breadth. This meant that the cold bit more fiercely into us, but at least we had air to breathe. We slept like a log until morning—our first peaceful night since arriving in Galati.

Chapter Three

The spring of '41 broke like a storm. A fiery sun as big as a cartwheel melted the ice in a few days; the icicles on the eaves sang forth the obsessive melody of falling drops. Many stores on the famous Strada Mavrogheni also seemed to liven up with the spreading warmth. Children came out of school in gaily spirited groups.

Father had found work with a certain Bitman, in a place that called itself a "luxury shoemaker's," on Strada Frumoasa. Some neighbors had helped Mother to obtain a cupboard and two chair frames covered with planks; they too served a purpose.

I had embarked upon various activities under Father's firm guidance. He brooked no discussion when it was a matter of school or the violin: he knew what was best.

But I have passed rather quickly over certain events from Bucharest in my mini-biography: I had come top of the class in my first grade at the Scoala Parfumului, where the headmaster, Mr. Popovici, had accepted me in spite of everything.

"The people at the ministry have only to tell me what they want. I can't bar any child from learning, even if he is a Jew."

This first teacher of mine had a son in the Iron Guard, who had to attend in silence the end-of-year ceremony at which I was handed my certificate, a parcel of books, and a garland of flowers brought from home. Mr. Popovici was a hardy type from the province of Transylvania, as strong as a fir trunk, upright, energetic, and very severe with the children. He had a special liking for me, because "he's a good boy and he can't help it if his name is Rose," as he said defiantly to some misguided parents who had requested a garland of flowers for their own children—and perhaps also my head on a platter. "It's a disgrace," I heard one of them protest in great irritation, "that a Jewish child should take the first prize away from us."

To be honest, even then I did not really understand what it was all about, nor did I attach too much importance to that voice, even though, sadly, it expressed the opinion of far more than just one individual.

As to the son in the Iron Guard, he caused Mr. Popovici a lot of trouble back home—as I discovered a little later from our neighbor Mr. Angelescu, the owner of a local bar, whose son sat next to me at school.

At home, I was considered a true hero. And what a hero! About that time I and several other children from my class took part in a magnificent festival in Carol Park alongside thousands of marching members of the royalist youth organization, the Sentinels of the Fatherland: a sea of little white berets, Sentinel kerchiefs, foaming horses, men in dress coats, flowers and hurrahs. A little farther off, King Carol himself sat on a white horse wearing a spiked steel helmet.

Mr. Popovici, with his typically Transylvanian calm, passed this test too when some backward parents indignantly asked:

"What is that Jew doing in the parade?"

"I sent the best ones for the march past. There they are."

My heroic qualities were especially appreciated by Father, who had never completed more than two years of primary school, although he had passed every class in the "school of life." He was intelligent, had an agile mind, and argued with faultless logic.

And, as I was saying, one of my father's great ambitions was that I should play the violin.

He was a real music fanatic, with a perfect ear, and he had learned a wide range of pieces by heart from a neighbor's radio that poured its waves through the trellis partition wall. He enchanted his friends, sometimes customers as well, with his repertoire of concerto fragments, lieder and canzonette, Romanian hora and sârba music, Serbian and Hungarian dances, and the never-failing songs of merriment *Bei mir bist tu sein* (You are so beautiful to me) and *Ot a Id a vabola* (A Jew has a wife).

One afternoon when I was playing a game outside—I shall never forget it as long as I live because of what it led to—he suddenly called me into his shop. Without asking me whether I felt like it or not, he put a flimsy little violin into my hands, a brightly polished instrument for children, and a little bow that I was told had been made from a horse's tail. It was that which fascinated and impressed me most of all at the time—a real horse's tail!

Then I was handed straight over to a violin teacher from Bucharest, Mr. Katevman, a Ukrainian Jew whose rather broken Romanian jarred on my ears, so that I often used to imitate him in fun. In return for the lessons, he brought his one pair of boots to be repaired every month, a huge pair with which he walked exactly like Charlie Chaplin.

My childhood was turned upside down and taken over by my study of the violin and of concertos for beginners by Robert Klenk, Sitt, Kreutzer and Viotti. I had some talent, it is true. But even after my first more accomplished scraping on the violin, my parents persisted in seeing me as a new wunderkind, after the model of Mozart, who at five or six gave concert performances that won him fame and glory—as well as money for himself and his parents.

"Come on, Mozart," I was goaded, half-jokingly but also half-seriously, "don't go to sleep with the violin in your hand."

The fact that Father was blocked from crossing the Danube to the Soviet Union and had to become an instant Galatian also contributed to his ambitions for me. He based everything on certain principles. As for school, "At least Licuta will have an education if I don't." Violin-playing was explained in terms of survival: "Even on an island, you can earn your living with the violin."

You must understand that I had started a strict work routine: mornings at school, then four hours of violin, one hard day after another.

What saved me and—can you imagine?—gave me a more pleasant life were the events that proved so bad for everyone else. Once German troops entered Galati, impressing everyone with their goose steps and their arrogant, stony faces jutting out from steel helmets, war preparations began in earnest and made themselves felt everywhere we turned.

Ration books were introduced for bread, along racially discriminatory lines, and huge queues became a common sight as food all but disappeared from the shops. On the other hand, platoons of Romanian soldiers noisily marched in step up and down the main streets, unaware of what lay in store for them. Jews were compelled to wear the yellow star on their clothing.

Thus, I had to spend many hours of the afternoon queuing for bread or baked cornmeal. Others in the line knew me and kept my place, while I went to play with the other children. My personal situation underwent a certain improvement, even though I grumbled about it.

In fact, I had begun to show signs of impatience: I did not like at all the "new life" promised by Father. I wanted to go home and be with my friends on Aleea Visini, to climb again the mulberry tree in the timber yard.

To calm me, Father formed an alliance with the Galatian violin teacher Mr. Leibovici, who soon became worked up and read "for my child's ears" something from a newspaper, prefacing it with a few words of his own:

"You pup, who keep whining after Bucharest," he started by saying, "just listen what Antonescu has got in store for you." And what he read did indeed put the fear of God into me:

"Beating must be introduced at school. But not every teacher will be able to perform it as he likes. It will be regulated beating, in front of the school and under orders from the headmaster. The guilty pupil will be undressed in front of the class and beaten on his back. A child is an animal and needs to be broken in. If he is not broken in, animal instincts will develop in the child."

War finally broke out in June. Swarms of Russian aircraft dropped hundreds of bombs on Galati. People were terrified. Strange though it may seem, however, the Russian bombs fell just right for me. We all went into the deep shelter on the corner of our street, and stayed there for hours on end until the all clear sounded. Then it was quickly-quickly back to my children's games. No one cared much about the violin any more—not even Father.

"Let him have some fun; he's still a kid. It's not the end of his days yet," Mother used to say, and Father had to agree.

I could hardly wait to hear the muffled hum of the Russian planes. I don't know why, but it happened nearly every day, between three and four in the afternoon, the very time when I was sweating with the violin in hand. As soon as the alarm sounded, everyone leapt up and ran to the shelter. Only I, ill weed that I was, remained in the house practicing Robert Klenk more diligently than before, until Father appeared and shouted at me as if out of his mind.

"Have you gone mad? Leave the violin there—come quickly to the shelter!"

But I complied with a show of reluctance and even dutifully took along the violin, much to my father's satisfaction. It was a rather sadistic game, which also kept my spirits up.

None of this should give anyone the idea that I did not like the violin. No! But I did hate the torture to which I was daily subjected, and the fact that whatever talent I had was measured by the number of hours I spent practicing, regardless of whether the sun was shining and all other children were outside playing, or whether there was thunder and lightning and the situation was different.

It is true that I even liked some pieces and played them very well on the violin. I shall always warm to Kreisler's *Frühlingslied*, the Mozart or Beethoven minuet, or the overture to *The Marriage of Figaro*. Light, transparent, melodious, uplifting.

The fascist regime of Antonescu became harsher for the whole population, but above all for the Jews. Camps and ghettoes made their appearance—those horrifying enclosures in which Jews, not animals, were forced to live.

Father was interned in the camp on Strada Frumoasa, not far from Bitman the shoemaker, in the main yard of a former secondary school. In the early days soldiers were on guard at the securely chained gate, but as things went from bad to worse they were replaced with presumably more reliable German troops. Abject poverty, hunger, humiliation, degradation: these words can substitute for any graphic description of life inside that verboten area. Each day mud-covered trucks left with a full load of prisoners—for what else were they?—to perform various kinds of forced labor: to dig trenches, canals, cesspits or shelters for the army. Twelve to fourteen hours a day. They returned at night completely drained of energy, cursed and beaten by the Germans. The *corvée* began all over again at crack of dawn. At home the food was coming to an end. We had used up nearly all of what Father had acquired in the last few months at Bitman's.

But again fortune smiled on us, in a different way. The Romanian army was beginning to develop its own workshops, and the larger garrisons were interested in having their own tailors, bootmakers, joiners, tinsmiths, bricklayers, painters and decorators—all, of course, highly skilled. They were not taken at their word but told to show what they could do.

Father delighted them with a pair of bison-leather boots, following a model made available to him in a German magazine Signal. The new boots, perfect in both design and size, were greatly appreciated by the exacting Colonel Dascalescu, commander of the Galati defenses, who asked after the "artist" responsible and ordered the Jewish bootmaker to be brought the next day to the battalion workshops—of course, under the labor regime practiced in the camps. There he worked, there he ate, and there he slept. He came home only on specially authorized visits, once every two to three weeks. For the rest of the time, it was just work, work, work: patent-leather shoes for officers' balls at the Military Circle, dainty little Parisian boots for their wives and mistresses, Bürger mountain boots, variously colored dancing shoes, and tiny footwear for their offspring. The size of the order varied with the officers' pretensions, tastes or whims. There was hardly a break from six in the morning until twelve at night, and when there was a great rush the work might go on until four in the morning. What did it matter if this meant toil and sweat and exhaustion? War was no joke: it required ever higher levels of output.

One morning, Father plucked up the courage to ask for more hands to be taken on in the workshop, arguing that he was no longer able to cope on his own.

The poor man did not know what he was letting himself in for. They sent him under guard to the camp on Strada Frumoasa to choose three more cobblers. Then the trouble started. There were some third-rate cobblers there, but all they knew was how to fix heel pieces and tips or, in the best case, to bury plated metal in the heel of a shoe. Perhaps they could have done that well enough, but that was not what it was about.

At that time, a chill of fear was sweeping the camp as the authorities were drawing up a list of Jews to be deported to Vapnearca, in Transnistria. Everyone waited in trepidation to receive the fateful announcement; everyone put on their talas and prayed more devoutly than ever, morning and night, for God to save them from this new trial inflicted on the people of Israel. No one knew how the deadly compilation was being put together, but many lists of names—some real, some invented, who could tell any more?—were already circulating in the camp and adding to the panic. And it was just as the decisive moment approached that Moses the shoemaker turned up to take three men for the army workshops.

As soon as they heard the great news, the mass of people became agitated by the hope of salvation and began to submit a flood of applications. One lawyer in the camp got a female member of his family to send my mother a hamper containing fresh fruit, a large piece of snow-white cheese, and a huge round loaf of Transylvanian bread, which was a rarity indeed in those days. Stuck with dough to the basket was a cryptic note: "From Mr. Smilovici the lawyer, wishing that God may help you for the good you do to others." When the "jewels" arrived at our home, Mother asked in amazement whether there had not been a mistake, and it was only after many assurances that she called out at the top of her voice: "The Lord has heard my prayer. It's a sign from above."

To be more precise, it was a sign "from below."

A teacher from another class waited for me a whole day to din into my child's ears the full drama facing his brother in the camp, Aron Herscovici. "Remember that name, my boy, and tell it to your father: Aron Herscovici. Not Sulim but Aron: the other one, Sulim, is another Herscovici who doesn't interest me."

In the camp, a leading member of the Jewish community sought out Father and asked him in a grave, official tone to recruit as his "cobblers" the deputy head of the local Jewish school, a rich man who financially supported the old people's home, and a kosher butcher who knew how to turn any chicken into holy food.

"All fine people," Father said impatiently, having realized that he had landed in a volcano. "But they are not cobblers. What am I supposed to do? The army wants boots and shoes. How can I make them with people like that!"

That evening he returned empty-handed to the battalion workshops between Lake Brates and the public gardens.

The next morning Major Bujor, a mild chubby type whose show of severity was meant to lend him authority at any cost, summoned my father to present his newly recruited cobblers.

"The only ones I found were useless. I need another day."

The major accepted the delay on behalf of the army administration.

The morning after, there was a veritable queue in front of the sentry box at the entrance to the camp. Dozens upon dozens of poor wretches were waiting to be accepted by Moshe the shoemaker, now promoted to the rank of "master" by his fellow Jews.

Everyone swore he had been a cobbler since the day his mother made him. But as soon as there was the least talk of "professional matters"—how to fix a piece of glenk metal, when to use Wagner nails or wooden ones, how to finish a double row of heel stitches—everyone shamelessly released a flood of irrelevant words, a flurry of nonsense that might have had some bearing on carpentry, masonry or tinsmithing, but not the slightest on the cobbler's trade. They shot out whatever came into their head, in order to save their own hide.

Seeing how things stood, Moshe had a serious chat with the top Jews on the camp committee and urged them to decide by the next day who should become a cobbler. All he asked was that they should be skilful people in their own trade, whatever that might be, and capable of quickly learning how to place a toe cap on a last, how to handle a counter, and so on.

In this way, Father thought, the headache would be passed on to others.

Towards evening, after careful consideration, they finally presented him with the three chosen ones: the highly capable kosher butcher, now shorn of his peies (locks) and beard, who had a fierce look in his eyes; an equally skilful jeweler, with his own workshop, whose voluntary contributions had ingratiated him with the Community leaders; and a respectable old man with black tortoise-shell glasses who had lived just across the way in the heroic times at the station shed, a lecturer in international law expelled from university and everywhere else for the same basic reason that he was a Jew. What kind of shoemaking could Father expect from such a man?

Nor was that the sum of Father's woes, for it has been known since antiquity that troubles never come singly. Confirmation of this truth came in the fact that the "list of three" contained another ten names: there were two lawyers; a professor of Hebrew; a lecturer in design and craft skills; the owner of a silkenware store arbitrarily taken from him by a former employee during the so-called "Romanianization" campaign; a pharmacist who had done a lot for his fellow Jews in time of sickness; a venerable usher at the synagogue who, though advanced in years, was still lively and alert; a half-paralyzed book-keeper who inspired you with pity as soon as you set eyes on him; a hairdresser who for some reason had the complexion of a young lady; and a thin, anaemic synagogue cantor who could barely stand on his feet. That was the proposed team of cobblers.

"Look, we were talking of three."

"You've got to find some way. Don't you want to help your own people when they're in a fix? Remember Haman and Esther in the Torah, remember the history of how your people have suffered."

After lengthy argument and supplication—and with the consent of mild Major Bujor, who understood many things without showing it—the army workshop took on not three but five "skilled cobblers" recommended by Master Moses, who tortured himself for quite a few weeks teaching each of them to carry out one operation more or less satisfactorily. The pressure of the struggle for survival left its mark on those poor wretched souls.

As any news traveled at the speed of light in the Strada Frumoasa camp, everyone immediately knew of the five new cobblers promoted by the Community. Some people, however, instead of feeling content that there were not just three but five, began to spread the vile slander that Moses had abandoned the others on the list as prey for the Germans. Poor Father soon became disheartened: the injustice of it all saddened him and reduced him to silence. He would never have expected such a thing in a million years. Instead of being thanked for the mitzvah, he was exposed to abuse. But what can you do? That's what some people are like.

In the end, someone slipped Father a discrete note in which the Community secretary Lazar Feibus invited him to come and see him in the camp. He thanked Father for what he had done, embraced him, and said that prayers had been said at the synagogue for his kind and devoted soul.

1941. Celebrating Purim in Galati under the directorship of Professor Davidsohn. Calmo Rose is the violinist on the left. He is nine years old.

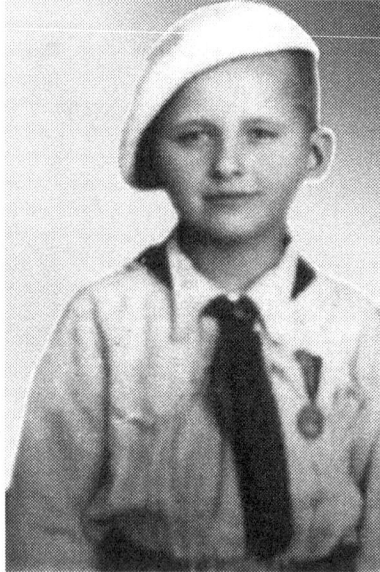

Calmo Rose dressed in the "strajer"
("Sentinels of the Fatherland") uniform in 1939/1940.

Father dressed in the Romanian army uniform,
the "Mountain Corps," in 1938-1940.

In Galati, in 1944. Returned from war, Gica (left), Father's aid, brought with him two sergeants and a warrant officer to recount war stories. They were photographed on the verandah together with Father and Calmo (on the right). Then they left, never to return.

The score for the operetta *Sylvia*. Written in 1942, in the Galati labor camp by professor Leibovici, it was used for the concert played by the Jewish orchestra from the camp for German and Romanian officers. The score is dedicated to Calmo.

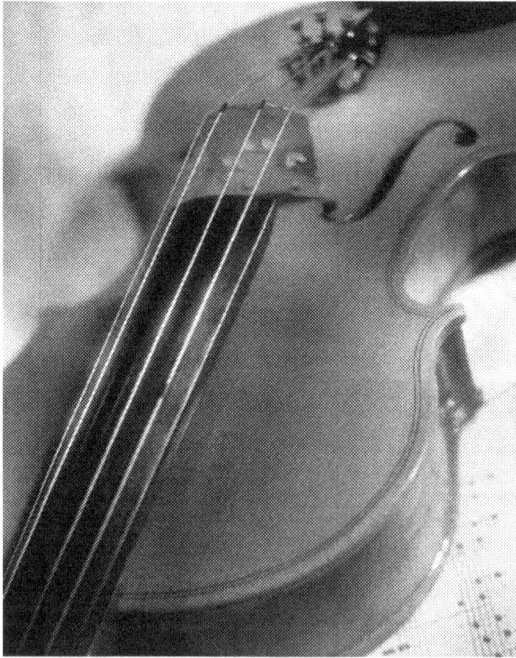

Chapter Four

During those terrible days I was eating my heart out for love of divine Luta. I did not know much about her: only that she was the daughter of a Jewish jeweler, Toporof; that she was intelligent and hard-working; and that—terrible to say!—once a month, usually on a Friday evening, some clever children aged the same as herself (who had to be prize-winners and to have passed their grade at school) were invited to a little party at her house under the watchful eye of her parents. Anchovy sandwiches were passed around, together with glasses of lemonade. They leafed through books and educational photo albums, and played at early version of Monopoly.

I had also heard that at some point, probably when they felt hungry, Luta's relatives left the children alone in the room together, and that the little boys and girls then joked and danced with one another. That made me especially bitter; the fact that they danced together. Some scurvy little kid, a complete nonentity, pressed the queen of my dreams to his chest, felt her breathe, and admired her smile just a couple of inches from his face.

I felt like screaming with rage. And I turned here and there, powerless to do anything about it.

I should have liked to be there too, in that room which I imagined to be just like Queen Elizabeth's in the film *Elizabeth and Essex* that was then being shown in Galati. Luta would be dressed in elegant period costume with a high lace neck, and I would be playing my violin, wrapped in something black with a gleaming sword at my waist. A child's day dreams.

Heaven knows how I tried to work my way into that noble home, but all my efforts ended in failure. I started out with certain disadvantages that were hard to overcome: I was a cobbler's son, and that didn't sound nice; I was not from Galati, I didn't know anyone there, and people called me "Lica from Bucharest" (which might just have worked in my favor, since it meant that I came from the Capital!). Worst of all, though, was the fact that I was not on close terms with anyone from the circle around the beloved object of my dreams.

Then I tried to find out who were her teachers. Someone whispered in my ear about her piano lessons, about the private instruction she had in French, and so on. I turned for help to Dulce, Ciuraru and even my odious rival Spielman, but it was all in vain. Not a ray of hope seemed to come from anywhere.

Then a little stratagem occurred to me: namely, to use the services of my violin teacher, Mr. Leibovici. I was the apple of his eye, as I was of his wife's, the woman who, for some reason, was always lying in bed and heartily sipping tea from a mug when I went for a lesson to their house on Strada Vadul Sacalelor. Well, my plan was that they should suggest to someone or other the creation of a Jewish orchestra in Galati. I would play Ciprian Porumbescu's

Ballade, at which I had recently been toiling away, and I would be accompanied by the orchestra and by Luta on the piano. This would allow me to get to know her, as we would rehearse together for hours at a time. My God, how wonderful it would have been!

I also imagined myself in the kind of tail coat that I had seen my idol, the enfant terrible Mickey Rooney, wear at the Rex cinema on Calea Dudesti in Bucharest. Luta would be in a lace dress with a train several yards long, just like the one that Elizabeth wore to the ball. Both of us would glow as we embraced on stage after the concert, receiving round after round of applause. Childish fantasies!

Dogged by passion, I no longer registered the grave events through which we were all passing. I had even forgotten that my violin teacher was no longer to be found at home on Strada Vadul Sacalelor, but was "living" in the camp.

How could I persuade the man in the camp's sentry booth, a Romanian conscript, to let me inside? I spent two days pacing back and forth in front of the silent, impenetrable iron gates.

On the third day, as I studied the "lie of the land" from my position on the sidewalk, I had a sudden illumination. I went straight up to the soldier and, in a tearful voice, delivered the lines I had thought up myself.

"Good morning, soldier." A short pause, then: "My father is here in the camp." Another pause. "He's fifty today and I'd like to . . . " I did not continue, so that he could see the pain that was tormenting me. I lied without any shame. Then, young though I was, I understood the devilish effect of an elliptical sentence that is suddenly left hanging.

The man looked me up and down and, I assume, took such pity on me that he let me through.

"Be quick about it—and don't be late back."

I shall never forget what I saw in the camp. I found many of my father's acquaintances changed in the face, with no appetite for life, skeptical and despondent. Clarenfeld, the neighbor with a grocery store, had gone crazy and was shouting for a woman to be brought to him—what for? I wondered—because he couldn't take it any longer. Mr. Klein, the plump pharmacist, was lying flat out on the stairs leading to the former staff room—and, to top it all, he no longer had any medicine for his diabetes and mumbled incoherently to himself. Others had found something to keep themselves busy: one was repairing some benches; some pious people were reading the Torah together; some young people whose faces burned from the swollen spleen of malaria were cutting worms into small pieces, while others secretly played poker with little stones instead of chips. All were ill, all had a high temperature.

Their clothes hung loosely from them. The air was filled with something sorrowful, an odor of slow yet certain decomposition. Probably that was what was intended.

I knew that Father was not in the camp. Around that time the treatment meted out to the Jews was becoming more brutal and derisive, and, as I said before, those fit for work were sent shoveling somewhere outside Galati and brought back to the "fortress" late at night.

What continued to obsess me, however, was something rather different. I had to find Mr. Leibovici to discuss the "business of the concert."

I found him at the back of a shed, where he was vigorously rubbing rosin into his magical bow of black horsehair. He had a troubled face, with large dark rings around the eyes that changed his appearance. He was a cheerful man in his way, who enjoyed writing down scores of overtures and even whole operettas that he knew by heart. I remember that before each lesson he would play one or another wonderfully melodious piece of music, which used to thrill me and for some reason to make me cry. I think it was from emotion, but also from despair. Perhaps I could see the gulf between the warm limpid tone of his violin and the false screeching notes that I still gave out. He played brilliantly pieces by Beethoven and Mozart, Paganini and Bruch, whereas my poor self offered paltry exercises by Kreutzer that grew obsessional through repetition. In my wretchedness, he appeared to me as a god. But now he would become my divine savior.

I was turning to him at a time that was crucial for me but most unhappy for him. I shot out the "official" version of my plan for the orchestra, without even mentioning anything about the "duet." He hesitated for a moment, then his face brightened and he passed sentence:

"It's a good idea!"

An orchestra would be welcome to everyone—both our people and theirs. Some more poor souls would be saved from the unbearable hard labor.

He began to think aloud. "Let's say we have three violins . . . two on the percussion . . . one viola . . . three wind instruments . . . as well as pianists and a double bass." Then he recited the names of all the Jewish instrumentalists in Galati, some professionals, others "amateurs full of good will," some in the camp, others in various "cultural reservations," which, as I learned years later, was the cynical term used by an SS officer in an interview with an International Red Cross magazine.

To everyone's surprise, it took a mere two days for approval to come down from army command—a speed that was somehow rather suspicious. I think they needed a little entertainment for their brave soldiers, who had just begun their retreat on the eastern front, without honors but probably with music.

There is no point in further describing the atmosphere that surrounded our local initiative. As soon as it became known that the orchestra was being formed, Mr. Leibovici was in turn besieged by dozens of applicants claiming to be expert at various instruments: the piccolo flute, the English trombone, the harp, the drums, and so on—none of which, as it happened, was available for them to prove their virtuosity.

"If you bring me the instrument, I'll show you what I can do," each one said, trying at all costs to be included on the list.

My teacher, a man of artistic temperament who had spent twenty years as leader with the Vienna Opera before fleeing from Nazi persecution, was little versed in the ways of the world and took each applicant seriously. But when he asked the military authorities in good faith for the instruments in question, they looked as if they had seen a ghost:

"We want an orchestra complete with instruments. . . . Stop hiding them and come and report back. Do you understand? Our battalions heading for Russia need your music. We want an orchestra—that's all that interests us. Is that clear?"

So that was how the heavenly vision of a Lica-Luta duo turned to naught. On the other hand, the military command had to be obeyed. You wanted an orchestra—well, find one! From a pleasant distraction, the whole thing turned into a nightmare.

All the "professional" musicians about whom anything at all was known—because they had once played at a baptism or a Christian wedding, for example—were summoned by the Community to rehearsals in the old school hall.

On the first day three violinists showed up and began to play whatever they could remember, creating an indescribable hullabaloo so that at least those outside could hear that the rehearsals were steaming ahead. But there were only three of them. That same evening, the members of the camp committee grew alarmed and kept searching until they found everyone on "Leibovici's list."

"Don't play with fire!" they said to them. "Things aren't too bad like this. What do you want—to get us all slaughtered? Go to the rehearsals, all of you!"

Through a series of dramatic appeals over five more days, an orchestra was slowly pieced together. Three men who had studied at the conservatory, plus Mr. Leibovici, of course, spent a few nights copying out instrumental scores, so that by the first Sunday Mozart's *Marche à la turc* was booming away and the first part of Kalman's operetta *Sylvia* was making satisfactory progress. The army needed happy, heart-warming pieces, which would have a positive effect on the troops in their shifting roles as liberators, oppressors, and conquerors.

But I have forgotten an important detail. I too participated in the activity of encouraging the army, playing second violin alongside two nice old men full of humor. They used to say:

"I'd happily go to their funeral! As soon as possible, God willing. The orchestra is ready for the burial feast!"

"Amen!" came the sung response of those who had heard.

One Sunday morning at eleven, when we were tuning our instruments, we suddenly heard the tramping of boots on the steps. The door swung open, and four officers appeared: three Germans and a Romanian. One of the Germans, perhaps more senior than the others, who had a two-hammer badge in his lapel and spoke some Romanian, thundered:

"Why are you making fun of us? Is that music?"

The reply, from strangled throats, was in the purest Yiddish, a kind of Tyrolean German, you might say:

"We are tuning our instruments. . . . We're sorry . . . "

Nothing more would come out; fear froze the words in their mouths.

"Ah . . . okay. I want to hear what kind of a funk you're in." And the German, rather friendlier than before, laughed at his knowledge of Romanian.

After a moment of painful silence, my teacher's mournful violin sprang to life and played the recitative music from *Sylvia* in heart-breaking tones. It was as if we could actually make out the words of the operetta, "Sylvia . . . Sylvia." The orchestra made a harmonious entrance—perhaps too strongly—and created the illusion of a live opera.

After a ten-minute "audition" during which no one spoke a word, the group of officers spun on their heels and headed awkwardly towards the exit. This time they closed the door gently. It was then that I first understood how music can tame even wild beasts.

I shall never know why, but the performance that our Jewish orchestra gave at the Military Circle for rookies, and even more for German and Romanian officers in the front rows, was publicized and announced from the stage as follows: "An orchestra will now give us a little entertainment." Not the slightest mention of our origin.

The concert was a success, even though one instrument or another often sounded unpleasantly harsh under the impact of emotion or fear. The hall was crammed full of bandaged "heroes," hobbling on crutches or lying on hospital trolleys, sobered down by the flame of battle.

At the rear exit our German acquaintance, the officer who had been spoiling for a fight, was waiting for us. In a metallic voice somewhat calmer than before, he offered us his thanks:

"*Danke . . . vielen Dank . . .* Orchestra play beautiful . . . *Deutsche Soldaten* very happy. Also play *Zimmer music*, duets . . . "

When I heard this request I nearly fainted. Here was a German officer, an enemy, carrying me into Luta's arms. He wanted ducts! Some members of the orchestra hurriedly assured him that anything was possible.

But again the train of life followed rails of its own, not those we wanted it to follow. At the next meeting of the orchestra I showed my interest in performing a duet with someone, and I even tested the water by pointing in a certain direction. Probably no one heard me, or no one took me seriously. The instrumentalists discussed the matter over and over again and eventually decided to form a trio of violin, cello and piano, its repertoire coming from a renowned German composer, Haydn.

"I'd also like . . . a duet . . . with someone . . . "

A hush fell over the room in what seemed to me an omen—whether good or bad, we shall soon see. People looked at me strangely. Then someone broke the silence.

"Well, yes, that could have an effect. A child, in a duet . . . "

I prepared to fill in the details: "A boy and a girl. Lica and Luta."

I experienced a moment of reverie such as I have rarely felt again in my life. But probably, the greater our happiness, the shorter it always is. My teacher, who loved me with all his heart, offered there and then to teach me to play Bach's double concerto with him. Imagine what he, the great hope of my life, was capable of doing to me.

Full of tenderness and good will, my violin teacher began over the next few days to carry out the execution; I received the score for second violin, which did not even strike me as too difficult. The nuances, cadences and rhythm, however, as well as the concordance with the first violin, could be mastered only through hours and hours of what seemed to me like slave labor.

I had to spend whole days of that summer vacation thrilling to Bach's divine music, so that I came to hate the sound of it. As I sweltered under the terror of that composer, he too a German, my "well-wishers" urged me on as if I were a boxer lying groggy on the floor.

"Don't forget: you're helping your own people."

The ferocious battles at Stalingrad and the ever clearer German defeats brought an icy chill even to the Galati region. The concert at the Military Circle where I was to be publicly sacrificed in the entourage of my enchanted teacher did not take place. They were no longer so passionate about music at a time when—to the great joy of camp inmates who heard the news via "I.P.A."—Russian guns and tanks were wreaking havoc in the ranks.

The I.P.A. news was then at the height of its popularity: any rumor that spread in the town, the camp or people's homes began with the hallowed words: "IPA reports that . . . " The story might be true, half-true, exaggerated, greatly exaggerated, or simply false, but it sounded a note of optimism amid that terrible war against the Russians and, so it seemed, the Jews. Just to make things clear: the three letters of the "people's news agency," freely translated, stood for *Idisches Plotkes Agentie*, Jewish Fable Agency.

In the end, the concert did happen—not in the public hall intended for it, but in a different place altogether. . . . But let me relate the exact course of events.

Once during that torrid summer Father did not appear at home for a couple of weeks; not a single sign of life. To make matters worse, I had managed to fall ill with a fever that sent my temperature soaring to 39 degrees. I had a headache, I could not eat, my belly was swollen, and I could hardly drag myself along. I was a victim of the Danube mosquitoes.

Mother was wringing her hands in despair. Left with no choice, she took me by the hand and set off for the battalion on the outskirts of Galati, somewhere beyond the public gardens.

"I'm looking for Moshe the Shoemaker . . . from the army workshops," Mother murmured, feeling intimidated by the rifle of the soldier on duty.

His reply was muffled by the noise of a dusty car trying to leave. Chubby Major Bujor got out and immediately understood what it was about.

You won't believe me, but he became more cheerful just at the sight of me, having heard from Father that I was a "musical genius," a new Mozart from Galati. He looked long and hard, then wrote out a prescription for me to take straight to the infirmary. There I was given a bag of quinine and a box of vials containing the liver extract "Hepacit" against my malaria.

They did not allow us to see Father, on the grounds that he was engaged in "major preparations for the units at the front." We felt excited when we heard those important words. Was he perhaps being sent to the front? I wondered with my child's mind.

We unraveled the mystery a couple of days later, when our man came home completely drained of energy. He seemed a different person—no longer my father. All his "comrades" in the shoemaking shop looked equally wretched. The war required footwear of all kinds, and that was no joke: footwear not for the soldiers dying one by one, however, but for the womenfolk and offspring of the top brass, who were preparing to celebrate Colonel Dascalescu's birthday in great splendor. The workshop had been given the choicest animal hides, the best-quality soles, buckles and finery—most of it probably war booty. In fifteen days of drudgery they assembled a grand total of fifty-five blockhouses—sorry, I mean fifty-five individual pairs of luxury shoes.

Well, anyway, it was not up to me to involve myself in army business. On the other hand, the army did involve itself in my business. And, as you will see, that was not a good thing.

I had made a favorable impression on the major, and he had even taken a liking to me. Seeing how I looked in the flesh—quite nice, why not admit it?—and remembering Father's enthusiastic words about my virtuosity with the violin, he formed the idea of giving the officers a little surprise at Colonel Dascalescu's birthday: that is, of bringing along me and my teacher, together with Bach the German, to give a live demonstration of my unique talent.

You didn't haggle with those people, however mild and honest they seemed. But the malaria was giving me no peace: in fact, it was giving me shivers, a swollen liver, and a nice high temperature. Even after intensive treatment with quinine and "Hepacit," the fever did not disappear. So the hard-pressed major, thinking of the anniversary in just ten days' time, gave Father three days' leave to use any way he knew to get me back on my feet.

"Bring him back to me alive and unspoiled," he joked. A contribution was needed from me.

Father listened to the advice of an old woman in the neighborhood, Leanca, who was barely eking out her days. So, he "operated" on me in the way handed down across the generations. He took me to a dreadful eating house in the main city market and ordered a "large rare steak," and with the greatest difficulty (because I had eaten nothing for a fortnight and become as thin as a rake) I was forced to swallow it down. He also made me drink quite a few glasses of red wine mixed with wormwood leaves, so that I was soon spread out with my head on the table. Then he took me back home, where I slept through until the next day. When I woke up—miracle!—the malaria had moved on to someone else. I was cured. The birthday show could take place.

Naturally I had to begin rehearsals again with my never-failing musical tutor, Mr. Leibovici. Warm gentle hours, bathed in expectation of finer days for others and for myself.

In the thick of the preparations, however, my schoolfriend Dulce brought me by word of mouth a wonderful piece of news that fell with all the force of a thunderbolt. Having managed to penetrate the "Luta network," he had arranged for a neighbor to speak with her parents about the new Mozart who had come with other émigrés from Bucharest—as a result of which I was invited on the second Friday in July to the girl's birthday party. A warm torrent of blood invaded my face and made me red as a beetroot. For a moment I thought my malaria had returned, but no, it was only that an immense joy had overwhelmed me. I would see her, be able to talk with her. . . . My heart beat violently, and a terrible pain kept stabbing me on the right side.

Imagine the dedication with which I plunged into the "military preparations," alongside my now dearly beloved teacher. Life seemed a bed of roses: I breathed deeply, enjoyed everything around me, and helped Mother with the cleaning until she wondered what on earth had come over me. I had become a good boy, mild and obedient, with a heart of gold. I lived in a world beyond Time.

Mr. Leibovici was proud to be showing those people his talent as a violinist and teacher, so that they could see for themselves what Jews were capable of doing. As for me, I was burning with expectation for the meeting at Luta's house, the "palace of my dreams."

Just when my joy was at its height, something quite unimaginable happened; it felt like a bad dream, more potent than if I and my whole family had suddenly been sent to the death camp then nearing completion at Vapniarca. At nine in the morning, Father announced that Colonel Dascalescu's party would take place on Friday at four in the afternoon, the very same time at which I was due to present my "letters of accreditation" at Luta's house. I could not believe my ears and asked for him to repeat it. He repeated it. A second later I was unconscious on the floor. They poured glasses of water over me, Mother shrieked with fright, and Father tried slaps to bring me round. This was sheer hell—what more was there to be said!

How was it possible? How could fate have dealt me such a blow? "Well, you see, it's perfectly possible"—I seemed to hear the devil himself mocking me.

I tried in every way possible to change the day or at least the hour. Who is the one to speak with?

I thought of falling ill, of swallowing a couple of pieces of chalk to raise my temperature, as my close friends advised. Okay, I would have been able to keep away from the colonel's party—but I would have had to miss Luta's as well. That wouldn't work. Either I was ill or I wasn't.

To whom can you say what is burning you up inside? Just when I thought my dream was about to come true, the devil's major forced me to spend the afternoon playing music.

On that fateful day I looked dark and sad, with eyes sore from weeping. No one could get on with me. Mother was the most dumbfounded of all: her dutiful son, who even swept around the house, had become a finicky, whimsical, unbearable child. I no longer did anything properly.

Four o'clock on that dark Friday found me in the state of a condemned man around whose neck a noose is being meticulously adjusted.

A large reception room, artificial daylight, clinking glasses, German gramophone music. . . . A company of officers reeking of perfume and dressed up to the nines stood around the birthday colonel, who was goggling back at them through his monocle. The excitement, fanned by glasses of *Cordon Rouge* and cans of Russian caviar, grew with each minute that passed. The soldierly hubbub was enough to split your ear drums. Everyone was speaking at the same time.

A little to one side, a group of highly respectful pearly queens prattled with a show of feeling among themselves; these were the officers' wives, who addressed one another in accordance with their husband's rank: *doamna colonel*, *doamna maior*, and so on. No one took any notice of my teacher and myself, although an orderly did serve each of us with a sandwich and a glass of soda water. Then we were given the nod by the mild-mannered Major Bujor, who had overnight become my personal enemy for the sacrilege of organizing this wretched occasion. In a good mood after several drinks, he announced in a triumphantly booming voice the presence of the two concert performers. Music stands, chairs, Mr. Leibovici and myself were brought in turn into the ring. A dull murmur spread around the room as it was realized how small I was.

"Look at the poor child," said an old and probably much-painted dame, one of those who want to appear younger at all costs. "How moved he is by it all!"

I do not remember how well I played, but the good humor of the officers and their wives was our guarantee of success. We were rewarded with long applause. The monocled colonel in person presented me with a large box of candies that had curiously twisted and inverted letters written all over it. Russian, Father said when he set eyes on it.

"Let the boy play something else for us," suggested my enemy, Major Bujor. "A solo piece, if he knows one."

"What else will you give us, dear?" a lady who was touring the room interrupted in the tone of a schoolmistress.

My teacher answered gravely in my place: "Next will be the Ballade by Ciprian Porumbescu."

I think that I put all my despair and suffering into the bow strings. Feelings of unhappiness elevated my soul.

Rounds of applause woke me from a daydream that I was with Luta's friends at her house.

Then the inevitable happened. Two rather befuddled senior officers—generals, I think, either Romanian or German—wanted to know the name of the talented youngster. Major Bujor, who, as I said, was a plain and simple man, told them the unvarnished truth.

An avalanche of insults crashed down upon him and shook the room. "How can a couple of dirty Jews have been allowed to sully a party of the army elite?"

I do not remember any more. All I know is that I lay awake that night, sad and unhappy, my eyes covered with tears of suffering that I could reveal to no one. I remained sick in bed for three days, with a high temperature.

I was dying of curiosity to find out how my absence from the goddess's party had been interpreted. After much investigation, I found a schoolmate who had been there. And what do you think he told me? No one noticed my absence. Only Luta was supposed to have remarked: "As for the guests who didn't show up, good luck to them." My guess was that she had been referring to me.

I had lost a great opportunity, a unique opportunity. But the passion in my heart never stopped growing.

Again I and my friend Dulce began to follow for whole days, wherever she went, the beloved girl from whom fate had so cruelly separated me.

Chapter Five

Summer passed, and autumn brought with its rainy countenance the well-known series of Jewish holidays.

One day Dulce slipped me a priceless piece of information: Luta and her mother would be going to the synagogue on Day X, at ten in the morning. "Let's sneak in there too. You'll look for the girl, talk to her and explain the problem you had with the colonel. That'll get things moving." Such was my friend's idea. I had a terrible shyness inside me and was quite unable to do anything of the kind—yet I did not completely dismiss the planned course of action. We'll see what can be done, there and then. I tried to be a little pragmatic about it.

On Day X, Mrs. Toporof and her dear daughter did not put in an appearance at that synagogue. We spent the whole day waiting there, to no avail.

Around that time, the young people of Galati were at it hammer and tongs with a kind of table football played with counters. Everyone had a famous team: Arsenal, Ujpest, Rapid Vienna, or whatever. In every house with children, the famous lokshenbreitl (kitchen boards for rolling noodles) had become football pitches marked out with variously colored pencils. The local "qualifying rounds" for the quarter-finals began more or less with the summer, in houses, yards and gardens, and on quieter street corners, from nine in the morning until everything was lost in darkness. And we kept this up for several days in the run-up to the "final." At least a hundred teams of this kind participated from every area of Galati: Tecucilor, Brailei, Badalan, Balaban, Cazarmii, and so on. Dramatic matches took place, with often unexpected winners. Everything hinged on the size and type of the ladies coat counters, and on the players' skill in precisely calculating the pressure to apply on each one so that it imparted the desired effect and recoil to the shirt counter serving as the "ball."

But let us return to the synagogue courtyard where we waited for Mrs. Toporof and her daughter. On the ladies' coats hanging there in the entrance, we came across some truly magnificent counters: large and concave, short and broad, square and tall, good for "moving upfield" or for "defense." All these player-bearing coats were heaped together on a kind of improvised stand, while the ladies themselves stood in their places on the first floor, separated from their husbands on the rows of rough-planed benches on the ground floor. We each managed to lay hands on a razor blade and had soon lopped off the large counters from a couple of overcoats. But then a one-eyed usher appeared from nowhere, and although he did not really understand what we were doing, an age-old instinct told him to stand watch in front of the coat stand. We waited for him to go away, but the man stayed put and prevented us from completing the football teams with the massive "players" from foreign lands.

Again it was Dulce who eventually came up with the solution: to move to the "tailors' synagogue" in a nearby street, which drew more high-class people and women dressed in proper overcoats, each with its set of "players."

Soon we were feasting our eyes on an impressive parade of coats, also left at the entrance to the synagogue, but this time without a guard. We set to work, carefully slicing off a splendid haul of "players" from as far afield as London, Vienna and Paris—for on holidays you went to the synagogue in your best clothes so that others would see you and realize you were not a beitler, a ragamuffin.

Cutting like good housewives, we made our way through a mass of coats, nearly the whole stand, and then vanished into the courtyard of Strada Columb No. 72 where we both lived.

First we spent a while sprawled in the grass, overjoyed at our feat. Then we called our friends from nearby to admire our latest batch: "players" with tall chests, of the most varied shapes and sizes and colors, in glass, stone and plastic. About noon, six of us set off like that to do a tour of the "house," oblivious to everything and everyone around us. What lunch? What house? We saw nothing, blinded as we were by passion and the exceptional value of our new acquisitions.

Not one of us heard the sound of the gate, the angry voices, the shouts, the curses . . .

It was Father who awakened us from our bacchanal—Father and five or six furious women, plus the one-eyed usher who showed that he had seen better than he was supposed to. Hands trembling with excitement swooped down upon our football pitch and seized the pick of our counters.

"You miserable children!" one of the victims said, ablaze with anger. "You've hacked our coats to pieces; you've stolen our counters. Shame on you!"

"What can you expect from cobblers' children—*beitlers* and *gonovs*," that is, ragamuffins and thieves.

There was a general scurry along the imaginary football pitch of the lokshenbreitl; each woman wanted to recover all three, four or five of her counters, because the loss of just one would spoil the whole set. I finally recovered my senses when a vigorous slap made me realize the stew we were in.

But there was worse than what happened to me. A few yards away, at the end of the yard, a country-style toilet made of wooden planks contained a large round ugly hole. Imagine my fright when Father, unable to stand any longer the women's fury, suddenly swept up all the remaining counters in his hands and flung them into the dark, foul-smelling aperture. What really hurt me was not the slap but the sight of my beloved players disappearing down there. . . . What a fate, the poor things!

The worst blow of all, however, was still to come. Who do you think was one of those she-devils? None other than Mrs. Toporof, who had lost to my blade not one, not two but all five of her Viennese counters—only a useless two of which she managed to recover before my Father's conclusive act.

There is no point in going on. Someone up there was obviously making fun of me. There was a plot against me—otherwise how could I explain the whole string of failures? I wept bitterly over the counters, but more painful still was that this would be the end of me and Luta. You can imagine what the girl was told about me.

I had to do something, to change the wretched sequence of hostile events.

Night had fallen, and Father had returned to his workshop after an unofficial leave for Rosh Hashanah. Dulce was suffering together with me.

"What if we tried to get the counters out from . . . down there?" I suggested.

"It's impossible. We'd stuff ourselves full of . . . " Dulce bluntly stated.

"Let's try all the same."

That night we devised an instrument of "salvation": a long clothes pole, with an empty can tied tightly to the end and perforated in such a way that any "stuff" that got inside would ooze out again. Ugh! There's no job worse than that of a cesspit cleaner.

The next morning, we went to the hole in question and moved the pole around for a while down among the gluey fetid liquid. When we pulled it back up, a foul stench swept us both off our feet. But we were young, hardy and persistent. We emptied the contents and—victory!—two large counters showed us their greenish visage. Without being seen, we quickly brought from indoors the bowl that Mother used to wash clothes and spent an hour or so splashing the pole and the stinking can inside it—until, finally, seven green counters smiled out at us. This time Providence was on my side, for among the seven saved from disaster were three dear counters belonging to Luta's mother. Praised be the Lord on high!

What we did not know was how to handle the olfactory side of things. However much we soaped and washed the counters, their original color never returned and their smell never went away. They stank to high heaven.

Then Dulce brought along a little bottle of his mother's "Coty" perfume and poured it over the precious objects. The resulting blend was a little more fragrant, a kind of bitter-sweet with a touch of choking ammonia. We washed them a few more times and continued applying perfume until it was somehow possible to breathe in their proximity.

Then we acted swiftly, in keeping with the parlous state of my feelings. We went to that old telltale of an usher, handed him the treasure, and asked him to take it to Mrs. Toporof with the message that Licuta "is sorry for the trouble and has done everything he could to get her counters back." To be sure that the usher would carry out his mission, we gave him a few lei that Dulce had produced from somewhere (as I was completely penniless).

So what did I hear after a few days? The lady in question thanked me and expressed surprise that I had been able to extract the counters from down there. Unfortunately she could not use them for various reasons, but she appreciated the gesture and my courage in going . . . and so on and so forth.

You might say I was a little rehabilitated.

Nevertheless, my obsession with Luta agitated me more than ever; all kinds of dark thoughts went through my head, including the frightening calculation that I had already chalked up two shameful failures. I interpreted the events with great passion: the girl, the queen of beauty, had wanted to have me beside her; she had broken through the barriers of the family Inquisition, which had wanted her to be surrounded only with children from "good families," but I, ungrateful wretch that I was, had not only stayed away from her party but failed to cover myself with an "official" excuse. Indeed, I had attacked her mother, stripped the ornamentals from the coat of which she was so proud—in the synagogue, no less!—and, having retrieved them from a cesspit, sent them back to her in what could only be described as a pitiful state.

Mother brought me back to reality one morning when she told me loud and clear that we no longer had anything to eat. Stalingrad was cutting the German troops to ribbons, the cold was causing their faith in victory to crumble, and their Romanian allies were showing signs of weariness.

These were the circumstances in which the "final solution" hurtled forward. In the camps of Transnistria, German technology was turning the racial dementia of Hitler and his acolytes into the reality of a merciless extermination of thousands upon thousands of Jews, who either ended up in crematoria or were transformed, with Teutonic thoroughness, into skin gloves.

It was hard to find a piece of bread in Galati, whether you were Romanian or Jewish. In that cruel winter, the wind blew with ruthless fury, driving along the white powdery snow. War brought hunger to the whole city. Romanian families waited in despair for death notices from the battlefront of a war that was not theirs. Long freight trains full of wounded soldiers pulled into the station only after nightfall, their drivers having been told to wait a few miles down the line.

"Don't panic me! Don't panic me!" the commandant shouted as he walked around the station noisily striking his boots with a horsewhip. Soldiers who lived in Galati or Covurlui were simply taken from the wagons and left to fend for themselves. Two or three hours later, around midnight, dozens of cripples and men still bleeding from head or stomach wounds flooded into Galati, some of them to collapse in the snow before they could reach home.

School broke up because of the lack of heating and teachers. Who could keep his mind on that any more?

And, you see, it was then that I became a violin teacher. I often used to say hello to a gentleman in our street, a relative of someone in the army who seems to have warmly recommended me to him. Well, this gentleman Enculescu, who was lame in one leg, claimed that his nine-year-old daughter wanted to learn the violin. And who do you think he wanted to teach her? None other than me!

I knew her from seeing her in the street, a pretty little Romanian girl. I had never paid her any attention. She could have been Aphrodite in person. I belonged to Luta.

But necessity can bend even steel in half—not to speak of hunger.

I was received with full honors at the gentleman's house, and I have to admit that I felt greatly flattered. As to the daughter, I think she was more cut out for the drum than the violin. She had no ear for music, no patience, no concentration—in short, she was a disaster. Most important for me, however, was that I was paid well. Mother and I managed to live on the proceeds.

After three or four lessons that were a torture both for me and for the poor girl, the father questioned me:

"So, is it going well?"

"It sure is! As you'll see. . . . " But I remember adding a note of caution: "You know, it takes years to learn the violin. We must be patient."

I think those good people would still be needing patience today if a Russian air raid had not destroyed their house and forced them to go and live with relatives in the country.

In any event, as I touched the girl's neck while adjusting the position of the violin, as I looked at her from in front and in profile, I felt something villainous growing inside me. A kind of carnal affection began to take shape for that tiny and—why not admit it?—dainty creature. By our third lesson I was encouraging her by stroking her head, cheeks and back—no more than that, I swear—and she was dying with pleasure. I thought of kissing her to see what that was like, but again my luck ran out. Just as I was preparing for that part of the lesson, after a game of languorous stroking, there was her mother suddenly in the room.

"What's going on, children?"

"Er, well," I stuttered, "I'm adjusting her violin—adjusting the position of its neck."

"Are you sure?" she added suspiciously.

I did not know what to answer. I kept quiet. Then I swept the violin from the girl's hands and started to play Beethoven's minuet (rather fretfully, it is true). And the muse of music came to my assistance.

"Beautiful, very beautiful," the music-loving mother pronounced, forgetting all about her accursed question. The difficult moment had passed.

Somehow, suddenly, I then began to reproach myself for what had happened. I loved Luta with all my heart, and there I had been on the point of kissing the little girl. What had come over me? I asked, innocent though almost guilty of the misdeed. And I realized that there is something very powerful inside man, a kind of irresistible instinct that sometimes comes to the surface.

Later, there came a second time when I saved the family ship from sinking.

The hungrier you are, the more brazen you become: this was a basic law that I did not yet know but to which I had already fallen victim. So one afternoon I presented myself to Mr. Grigorescu, the owner of a little "family restaurant" on Strada Balaban, and offered to create "a family evening atmosphere geared to these difficult times of war." Maybe my language was influenced by Pearl Buck's *Mother* and *East Wind: West Wind* and Camil Petrescu's *First Night of War, Last Night of Love*, which had made a deep impression on me.

Without much ado, he stared at me for a long time and asked me to show him what I knew. I took my violin out of its case, with a calm and serious air of self-importance, and gave a fiery performance of a few tunes that were stirring Romanian hearts at that time: *Du-ma acasa mai tramvai* (Take me home, streetcar), *Lampagiu de altadata* (Lamplighter of old), *La casuta alba* (In the little white house), *Mi te-ai lipit de suflet* (You've stuck to my heart), and finally a war song *A plecat la vânatoare Agarici* (Agarici has gone off hunting). (Agarici was the name of a Romanian pilot said to have shot down I don't know how many Russian planes.)

He nodded approvingly and said I should start enchanting his customers at eight o'clock that very evening. We clapped hands, as it were, and agreed that I would be paid daily one loaf of bread, one hundred grams of salami, five olives and a pickled vegetable. It was a very good price for those times of shortage, cold and insecurity.

I went there for three evenings, and the place did seem to liven up. The fourth evening, however, proved to be my undoing. At one table some thirsty souls were drinking themselves senseless, with glass after glass of a sweet-smelling anisette. They talked loudly, almost barking at each other, and at one point a short swarthy man let out:

"Antonescu is the man for the Jews. He got them out of the army and everywhere else so they wouldn't have to go to the front. Our people are dying while the yids stay under cover."

My child's mind told me that I had never heard anything so stupid in my life. Without thinking where I was or who they were, I found myself shooting my mouth off.

"But they've been shut up in labor camps, where they go hungry and sick. They've been handed over to the Germans, who are killing them at Vapnearca and other camps in Transnistria."

"Shut your trap, you little yid boy. Clear off out of here."

And they were just about to start hitting me when the landlord intervened. He thrust the violin case in my hands, gave me my daily packet, and asked me nice and friendly never to set foot there again.

"That's what our Romanians are like. They repeat every stupidity they hear from others—from the Iron Guard."

And I could not help remembering the scene from my first year at school, when a number of parents blamed the director for giving the first prize and garland to "the little yid boy." The same words!

Are they all like that? I asked myself.

Fate has made me realize that, after all, there are people and people. Some have darkness inside them, like those men in the restaurant. But there are also decent unprejudiced Romanians, like my father's bosom-friend Gica, the shoemaker from Strada Tepes-Voda, who was conscripted and seemed to disappear without trace.

As chance would have it, a great surprise was in store for us. The boot workshop was strengthened with a couple of Romanian soldiers, both "good shoemakers," as Major Bujor announced a few days before their arrival. And when Father looked up from his last, who do you think was standing there? It was Gica, the same decent guy to whom Father had once taught the trade. What a great joy it was! They hugged each other, looked at each other with tears in their eyes, exchanged words of encouragement.

A few days later, on a Sunday, they came back to our house—not alone, though, but with two sergeants and a warrant officer. We all had ourselves photographed together on the verandah.

Of all Gica's stories from the war—they were in Galati only for "rest and recreation" before returning to the front—the one that made the strongest impression on me took place in the trenches. His company was about to move out under fire, when Mihnea, a man from the same village as Gica, tried to keep their spirits up in his normal jokey way. Unfortunately, what came out was: "We're going to die, lads, that's for sure. But I've been preparing a surprise for the general. I'll get them to write on my gravestone what someone I knew got written on his. When you come you'll read: 'Here I lie and here you read. I'd have preferred you to be lying and me to be reading.'" The men all burst out laughing, and then suddenly the voice of Captain Costea roared out from nowhere: "Have you joined the Bolsheviks, you bunch of lepers? Making fun of the flower of the Army?" Crash, bang! No one knew exactly what happened. Mihnea got hit by a bullet that left him lame in one leg. Gica had one of his hands crushed. When they came round, all hell had broken loose. They were thrown into a goods wagon. For three days and three nights they were left to rot—until they were finally taken for "recovery" with the other wounded.

Gica left again for the front, and this time he was gone for good.

Chapter Six

In all my bustle to survive, my pure thoughts were directed towards Luta. I wanted to see her again, to strengthen my faith before her icon.

Again I lay in wait on the corner of Strada Brailei—not alone, but with my old schoolmate and companion in suffering, Dulce.

In the space of a few weeks, the girl had blossomed into a gorgeous young lady whose stamping heels echoed down the sidewalk and, more to the point, made my heart race with the sickness of love. I watched her discreetly from the other side of the road or, if I was behind her, hesitantly followed her scent. I imagined that she felt my presence, as from time to time she stopped for no apparent reason other than for me to catch up, and then resumed her diaphanous flight.

Not once did she come out alone. Always she was accompanied by her mother, a female neighbor, or an older friend of the family. But I and Dulce formed a silent escort, to which I assumed she had grown accustomed. So we had some "activity," thank the Lord.

Once we waited three whole days in vain for the goddess to appear. What had happened? We only knew her daily schedule. We did not realize why a discreet silence was being woven around her.

One afternoon I saw the school doctor enter Luta's house—a venerable old man with a white beard who, in keeping with his character, had a slow and methodical gait. He reappeared after an hour or so, with the same expression on his face from which it was impossible to read anything. I took my heart in my mouth, crossed the street, and with unparalleled courage offered him my respectful greetings and tried to strike up a conversation. I told him I was Rose from the third grade, and he recognized me.

"You're the boy with the violin, aren't you?"

"Yes, doctor."

Rather awkwardly cutting short the discussion on musical themes, I then asked him about the subject that was paining me.

"Have you been to see Luta? Is she ill?"

"The poor girl; her temperature has hit forty. She's got paludism."

"Paludism? What's that?"

"I mean malaria, fever."

Stung by the news, I left the doctor rather too abruptly. He would have liked to continue chatting.

I knew from my own person what it meant to be struck down by that wretched malaria. Besides, I was convinced that I was the only one in the world who could make her recover, thanks to the medical secrets I had learned from Old Mother Leanca. The experiment had produced splendid results in my own case, so I had indisputable competence in the matter.

The only problem was one of—communication. Luta's mother had to listen to me, to believe me, and above all to apply my treatment. I was sure the doctor would oppose it and recommend further injections of "Hepacit" and quinine, quinine and "Hepacit," right up until the girl passed away, God forbid!

"What shall we do, Dulce? We must do something fast to save her. But what can we do?" I kept repeating in desperation.

That night I did not sleep a wink. The hours crawled by, but my mind was burning to find a solution.

Why should we lie? The truth is the best lie—my Mother used to say. So the next morning, having taken along Dulce as a shield, I rang at the Toporof house at nine o'clock. With the boldness of a lunatic. Once, three times, ten times.

A woman who was not Luta's mother finally appeared at the door, obviously a little frightened by my persistence, and asked me what I wanted. I answered in a single breath.

"I know Luta is ill and I want to recommend a certain cure. It's a secret of mine."

"Are you in the same class at school?"

"Of course."

"The poor little thing is really very ill," the woman finally said. "The doctor came and she's having daily injections, but the temperature still hasn't gone down."

"That's the point: I know a more reliable cure. I once had malaria and I shook it off in one day," I blurted out without pausing.

My information seemed to interest her, as she asked for details. I told her of the "treatment" that had cured me so quickly: the tavern at the New Market, the steak dripping blood, the mug of red wine with wormwood, the pickle, the restful sleep, and the next day's miracle. By the time I had finished, the woman had already retreated back up the two steps in the entrance. She thanked me awkwardly and only wanted to know who she should say had brought the cure.

"I am Lica, the violinist from Bucharest—please tell Luta that," I continued with the same self-assurance.

She ushered me out into the street, with an exaggerated show of respect. Why did she keep looking at me all the time?

My "good deed" had an epilogue. Dulce conveyed to me the words of Luta's mother, which he had heard by the mysterious ways of the Lord.

"That boy has got something in his head about our family. He follows my daughter in the street for days on end, as if he were quite mad. He steals the counters from my coat. Now he comes and suggests poisoning my daughter. And to think that he is a Jewish kid!"

I had not been expecting anything like that. All I had wanted was to . . . to do what?

Again the Almighty had hurled thunderbolts at me for my reckless approach to Luta. It felt as if I was under a spell that I could never break, however much I tried. I was sad, angry, disappointed, and other things besides. My state was like that of someone who, despite his efforts to reach shore, keeps being driven further away from it. I suffered inside myself and wept secret tears.

Not long afterwards, we had other reasons to shed bitter tears. Russian tanks had overwhelmed positions held by German and Romanian troops and were preparing to cross the Dniester. Galati itself seemed about to fall any day. Many people were killed during air raids, when hundreds of bombs were dropped at random on houses, factories, military units and anti-aircraft batteries. Everything was closed down, the streets were deserted, houses on fire, hospitals crowded with the wounded. Fear and panic took hold of the city, which was like a place under siege. The Russian prisoners held at Gallus paint factory took advantage of the confusion to flee wherever they could.

Once the army guards had vanished from the camp gates on Strada Frumoasa, those still interned there made haste to liberate themselves and return home. They could be heard vigorously shouting: "The Russians are coming, we're free!"

Could anyone of sound mind have thought otherwise at the time? The numbers in the camp had already been reduced a week before, when many of those who had arrived on the emigrant trains in 1940-1941 and been classified as "Communist," or not even that, were brutally shipped off to a destination no one knew and from which no one ever returned.

But what of Father? Where was he? Broken by the daily grind, all the craftsmen were sent to workshops on the edge of town and made to continue fixing soles and sewing tops on the shoes of intransigent officers who believed in their cause right to the end.

He came home at night, secretly. He and others had risked their lives slipping out of the garrison, afraid that they would be caught and executed just as the whole show was about to fall apart. Father too had profited from the waves of bombing that were shaking the city to its foundations.

We scarcely recognized him: he was just skin and bones.

The next morning at six, the sirens began their terrible wailing. While we bundled into the shelter and descended some fifteen meters down a narrow flight of steps, Father remained in the cellar opening to see what was happening. Just then a Russian bomb fell from the sky and sent him somersaulting onto the steps, where he was left with his loins crushed to cry desperately for help. Help? Who and from where? He lay indoors for several days until the Russians had occupied the city, and by a stroke of luck they set up an army medical post just across the way on Strada Cazarmii.

Mother stayed at home, hidden at the bottom of the yard. The "triumphant" entry had been followed by a wave of vandalism that was hard to imagine. There were stories of Russian soldiers who entered houses and requisitioned clocks, bottles of perfume (which they drank) and other things. And although we said they were lies, we were still afraid and thought it better to be safe than sorry.

I had one hope, and with this in mind I crossed the street to where the Russians were. A soldier on guard with a fur cap pulled over his eyes looked me up and down incredulously. As there was not enough room inside for all the wounded, a number of large tents had been raised around the building. Someone in the yard noticed me at the gate and called out: Idi syuda (Come here). He behaved in a friendly way towards me, giving me some chocolate that I immediately wolfed down. I was starving. He kept talking to me in a gentle voice, but I did not understand a word. He took out a sepia photograph on which I could recognize him, the soldier, with a fairly young woman and three little children. The photo had a wide black band around the edges. He stroked it and cried. Probably his family had been killed by the Germans.

But I was worried about how to help my father and did not have time for such scenes. I explained in gestures that I lived across the street, and that my father was ill in bed. I don't know how, but the man understood. He called someone by the name of Ivanov, who went home with me and, finding Father in bed, immediately grasped the situation. Then Father said a few words to Mother in Yiddish, explaining that the Russian seemed a good man and that she should not be afraid of him. And believe it or not, the Russian understood.

"I'm also a Jew. I'm a doctor . . . at the hospital they use me just as a male nurse."

"Why's that?"

"Because . . . "

There was a short pause and the man hurried out. Twenty minutes later, a dusty old military jalopy took Father to the Sfânta Maria civilian hospital, from which he hobbled back a fortnight later.

At two o'clock on the morning after Father went into hospital, our front door was banged open by two blind-drunk Russian soldiers who could scarcely stand on their feet. They turned the house upside down, screaming that we were "bourgeois." I was alone, but for some reason I did not feel afraid. They had brought with them two large pickle-containers filled with a strong spirit, and all the time they drank enormous glasses of the stuff. Everything stank of alcohol.

"*Gde khozyaika?* Where's the lady of the house?"

Mother had hidden herself again at the bottom of the yard. Much later, after they had sung or bawled a number of sad or quarrelsome songs, they collapsed with their heads on the table.

I don't know what time it was when they finally scuttled away, leaving everything behind in an indescribable mess. Broken glasses, plates crushed with the heels of their boots, salami rind, half-eaten cans smelling of cheap brandy.

This was the first tear in the idyllic picture of Soviet Russia on which we had concentrated all our hopes of a better and juster life. "For these liberators to enter your home blind drunk, to turn everything upside down, to sow terror around them so that you are afraid to show yourself . . . "

Days passed, but Mother was too afraid to put her head outside until Father returned from the hospital.

Again I crossed the street, this time together with Father, and we tried to find Ivanov the nurse to thank him. They let us enter the Russian camp, where there was a strong smell of creoline. Ivanov took Father to one side and whispered something to him. By the time we left I was holding some large cubes of chocolate with a punched indentation, while Father was carrying an army loaf, some biscuits and Neapolitan wafers.

Back home, he immediately called Mother and said something to her that really put the wind up me. All his dreams had turned to ashes.

"Ana, things are even worse over there. This Ivanov is a Jewish doctor, whose real name is Ghersensohn. He landed in an unit made up almost entirely of Ukrainians, as anti-Semitic as they come. Yes, you heard right: anti-Semitic. All over Russia the Jews are harassed and persecuted. Before the war they were removed from their jobs and sent to camps—because they have those there too. Some were even shot after a trial. Nearly all the Jews have changed their names so as not to be identified and tormented. Doesn't that all sound really great?" And Father heaved a deep sigh.

When a polkovnik, a Russian colonel who had seen him in the camp, called him over to have a word with him because he had heard he was a saposhnik—that is, "a cobbler, like Comrade Stalin"—Father presented himself in a way that left me flabbergasted: "first name Misu, second name Rosu." Yes, he too was disguising his real name. There no longer seemed any point in going to Russia, if Jews there were given a hard time and had to change their names.

Medical assistant Ivanov, alias Ghersensohn, also drew a grim picture of Birobidzhan, the so-called national home of Soviet Jews, which was a kind of huge camp where everything was rationed by the gram and centimeter for 12-14 hours of work a day. Not a single normal Jew had gone of his own free will to the Soviet Far East—the only ones to leave were those who had received a sentence, or else so-called "devoted" Party members who, having no other choice, had thought it fit to play that role.

We could not believe what we heard. Father cried, Mother cried, Ivanov-Ghersensohn cried—and I too tried to cry, not so much because of the story as from family solidarity and a spirit of imitation. I still did not grasp the horrors about which they had been talking. Father then thanked the Good Lord that we had never managed to cross the Styx.

So, something worse is always possible, I said to myself, now a little more mature because of the various experiences I had been through.

But how did things stand with me and Luta?

The tumult of war and my family's sufferings had by no means quelled my enthusiasm. In May or June, when the bloody battles were reaching their height, my mind was not only on school. As I stood watch beneath the balcony, I the little Romeo forgot all about school, classes and teachers.

Well, then came trouble. Our teacher of Romanian and history, a very special man called Davidsohn, who could be strict or gentle according to the circumstances but was always keen and inspired when he spoke to us, had somehow guessed where my mind kept wandering.

One morning, sensing that I had not done my homework although I was the winner of the class prize, he asked me directly:

"Have you written the composition?"

"No."

"And why not, may I ask?"

"I forgot."

"So why have you come to school?"

"To tell you," I joked, trying to improve the situation. After all, I knew the teacher had a sense of humor.

"That's good, a good reply." He hurried to his desk to note something or other down (why, I could not say) in a thick notebook with a chestnut-brown cover. Then he informed me in a gruff voice that he had put a big "3" against my name in the class register—and he sent me out.

In the next break he tracked me down in the corridor and, staring me in the eyes, threw me completely off balance.

"Is it because of Luta?"

Silence. Then, finally, between my teeth:

"Yes."

"Do you know her?"

"No."

"Have you spoken to her?"

"No."

"Does she know you?"

"No."

"Has she spoken to you?"

"No."

"Do you . . . love her?"

"A lot—like Mother."

I had told the whole truth.

I remember being surprised that he did not lecture me. Instead, he looked down at me with something like pity and shook me with his grave baritone:

"Be a man, my dear boy. Be a man!"

And to his honor and my own gratitude, he never said a word about all this in front of the class.

The cold shower seemed to awaken me from a dream.

"Why should I be cowardly and let myself go under? I'll tell Luta what I have on my heart. I'll be a man."

Once the Russians entered Galati, my attempts to conquer the girl of my dreams seemed to gain fresh momentum. The martial spirit of the times evidently had me in its grip. I even stopped using the services of my good friend Dulce and took my fate in my hands.

Lonely and disconsolate—that's how I was—I took up position on the street corner and again began to follow her everywhere: to the butcher's and the baker's, to her Hebrew classes where I waited outside for two hours, to her Romanian teacher who was too ill to travel himself, and so on. Whether she saw me or not, I do not know—nor shall I ever know. I felt I was choking. She, on the other hand, grew more beautiful with every day that passed. My God, what eyes! what laughter! what a snub nose! Why go on? Everything about her was magnificent.

I said to myself that the time had come to stop her in the street, to introduce myself in a straightforward way, to tell her that . . . that I loved her with all my heart; that I dreamed of her at night; that I wanted to be her friend; that I was a good boy; that I could no longer live without her.

It was a Wednesday evening when I finally decided to clarify the situation the next day. At home there was talk that we would soon be moving back to Bucharest. I whispered to Mother that there was a girl, Luta, whom I liked a lot and wanted to visit. She did not even blink, bless her. She got me ready as if for a holiday festival: white shirt, pink tie, long trousers (an event in itself, as they were the first I had ever worn).

I plucked up courage and lay in wait from ten in the morning until late in the evening. No light in the window, no movement inside. What could be going on?

The next morning at seven I was back in front of the house. But I waited in vain. There was no one. Around midday someone stormed into Luta's house and came out with an upholstered chair. After another hour, the same person returned and took away another chair. I could endure it no longer and asked him about the Toporof family.

"Bah! they left a couple of days ago. Relatives in Vienna."

I reeled back white as a sheet and burst into tears.

"That's impossible! Impossible!"

"What's the matter with you, kid?"

But the shock just made me keep repeating mechanically: "That's impossible . . . impossible!"

It was already evening when I reached home, red-eyed and drained of energy. Mother put me straight to bed and rushed to bring me an aspirin.

"What's happened to you? Did you see her? Did you say goodbye? But you're ill, my pet."

Yes, I was ill, very ill indeed.

Since that day, whenever I have seen a face that resembles Luta's, I have trembled and felt my heart flutter—at the age of sixty-five as much as at twenty-five. No one has been able to prize her out of my heart. Not even Dulce.

But why do I mention Dulce? Years later, someone told me that my old friend and classmate had gone like the Toporof family to Israel, that he had married the Luta "he had loved since childhood," that they had children and grandchildren, and that . . .

My God, what did I do to deserve it?

Lost in thought, I stand and listen to the lament of the violin, whose trembling voice rises up close by.

www.ingramcontent.com/pod-product-compliance
Lightning Source LLC
LaVergne TN
LVHW011411080426
835511LV00005B/478